A Mother's Love

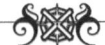

A Mother's Love

A Foster Mother's Life Time Experience

By Velma M Stewart

Order this book online at www.trafford.com
or email orders@trafford.com

Most Trafford titles are also available at major online book retailers.

Printed in the United States of America.

ISBN: 978-1-4269-6013-0 (sc)
ISBN: 978-1-4269-7681-0 (e)

Trafford rev. 12/16/2011

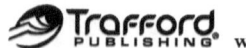 www.trafford.com

North America & international
toll-free: 1 888 232 4444 (USA & Canada)
phone: 250 383 6864 ♦ fax: 812 355 4082

Dedicated to:

My Husband Donald G. Stewart
And to all my children; especially Shalanda, DJ, and Eric

.

ACKNOWLEDGEMENTS

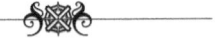

There are a number of wonderful people who encouraged me to write this book. My gratitude to my family, especially Auntie Dr. Edith Hines, Mavis Burns, Carolyn Moore. To my late Pastor Bishop Charles Thomas from Victory in Christ Church he gave me confidence and encouraged me to continue with my book no matter what. With this encouragement I will always appreciate their love and support.

Foster Parent's Prayer

Heavenly Father show me the path that leads to being "The Best Foster Parent" and help me journey through the good times and the bad. Help me to understand my foster children as I would my own; to listen to them carefully when they have something to say and answer their questions to the best of my ability. Help me to be strong and to hold my head up high to be looked upon by my foster children as a constructive influence. My I accept them for what they are and not for what they could be? Show me how to teach them right from wrong and that being honest leads to a better life filled with happiness and joy. May I grant them the right to make some decisions for themselves and to learn to accept responsibility? When I am angry or upset, help me to control my temper; and shall I not punish them to show my authority over them. Help me to prepare them for when they leave to deal with life's uncertainties. Amen

I think this was to be a guide. I only remember hearing this prayer one time at our first meeting. Other prayers of our own choosing were followed at other times. We were asked to meet once a month after supper. For me, it was a short walk down the block. Sharing a prayer time together set a tone for our guidance from the agency. Each parent would share a moment of their time with their responsibility. The children's behavior was a prominent conversation. The group interaction showed us the different ways of handling each child's behavior. The children are looking for love!" showing temper, teasing and getting on your last nerve. Example one of my ten year old was constantly telling me I wasn't his mother and that I was ugly and that I could not cook. After his tirade he would laugh and point directly at you. The foster parents would be reminded that they were to be accommodating to the children's needs.

A Mother's Love

A mother's love is unconditional. She will do without just to make sure her children are well taken care of. A mother comforts her children. She loves her children even when she has been hurt by them. She realizes, she can't give up now but must keep her faith and hope for the best. She sometimes feel like all hope is gone but realizes that with prayer, fasting, reading God word and asking God for understanding she can make it. No one said it would be easy raising children. There is going to be ups and downs that we must go throw. A mother can't throw in the towel on her children because she knows help will be on the way. The bible tells us to ask and it will be given to you; seek and you will find; knock and the door will be open to you. For everyone who asks receives; he who seeks finds; and to him who knock, the door will be open. I believe if I do ask seek and knock I will find help for my children when in need. There is someone who has more experience than you do when raising children.

As a mother you must keep yourself available at all times for your children. I don't mean put your life on hold but do the best you can for them. A mother knows her children even when they think she doesn't. A mother knows the voice of her child. She knows when something is wrong by the tone of her child voice. She knows even if that child doesn't say a word. She knows by the look on her child face. A mother is precious; there is no amount of money that can buy a real mother love for her children. A mother seeks wisdom. She trust in the lord with all her heart, and she leans not on her own understanding but ask the lord to help her with her children, if she does that then God shall direct her in the right way.

A mother will always love her children in good and bad times; just as our heavenly father loves us we must love our own the same way unconditional. A mother's love is real, you can tell by the things she does. You can feel her love for her children even if she doesn't say "I love you" she shows it. For the nine months she carried you inside up until you became a young adult. She still took care of you and there is no charge for loving you the way a mother do. A mother's love will never die. She will take that love to the grave with her.

Contents

Introduction

Title: A Mother's Love: A Foster Mother's Life Time
        Experience

I had fifty-five foster children in five years. This was due to
me taking in siblings' group so the children could all stay
together. The experience I had before becoming a foster
mother was helping raise my six siblings. My husband
and I have two children of our own. I joined an agency
in Brooklyn, N.Y. to become a foster parent. The agency
was Miracle Makers. The Miracle Makers required you to
take classes in order to become a foster parent. After taking
classes and you have passed the requirement, they would let
you know if you will be getting children in your home. My
home passed the requirements. Some of the requirements
were: Have a regular income. A background and a criminal
check on everyone living in the home. Administration
Children's Services was checked to make sure that we didn't
have a case against us. Good health was required and also
being medically cleared before any child enters our home.
Most important was my desire to help those in need. To take

children for money and not because you love children and want to show love to those children who never knew love in the home would be detrimental. After having a child in your home for two years or more you fall in love with that child and it's hard to let go, when it's time for that child to return home to his or her family. You are told not to get attached. But how can you not become attached? As a mother it was very hard not to get attached to the children that are in a family situation twenty four seven (24/7).

It was not easy being a foster mother because the children didn't allow you to help them at first. You have to win their trust; you need a lot of patience. The children test you in every area. They would make up untruth to the caseworker. Most times the caseworkers believe them. The caseworker won't tell you anything the children told them. However sometimes the caseworker acted as if you have committed a crime because of what the children told them. The workers would come to our home unexpected in trying to catch you unaware.

You had to be confident in yourself and be yourself. I find small children were easy to deal with especially ages of ten months to five years. They do not know right from wrong so they have to be taught. If a child stayed with you for about a year when the time comes to go home it is hard for that child as well as for the Foster parents and other children in the home at the time. They don't understand why they must leave you. Sometimes you explain it to them but they often times feel they did something wrong.

I feel children are a gift from God. I say this because there are people who want to have children but cannot. As a foster mother I was a fill-in until their mother got her act together.

I was not trying to take the place of their natural mother just a helper until their mother got it together. However, when you are around children every day you become very attached to them. You feel as if they are your own.

I thank God for allowing me to be able to help other children beside my own. This experience also helped me with my own and showed me how to become a stronger mother for my own. Added to this new experience was being with Haitian, Jamaican and Cuban families. The only common denominator was that we all had colored skin. Now would be able to share the American experience.

Why Did I Become a Foster Parent?

I became a foster parent because I wanted to give back to the children that needed a good home and never knew what a home of peace and love could be like. I worked for administration children's services and saw how so many children came in from different home settings and was seeking for someone to love them and accept them for themselves. Many times those children were put out of their own homes due to a lack of understanding along with disobedience also children were put out due to parents abuse, neglect, and drug abuse I felt if I could just make a different in one child life it would mean so much to me just to know I did my best in trying to help in the community. If I succeed with one I believed I could go a little further and hopefully set an example in my home for others to see they can have peace of mind and learn how to love one another.

My husband wanted us to have foster children. He was once in foster care he and his siblings. He was separated from his six siblings and even his identical twin brother. He wanted to give back some of the care and love that was given to him. He had a wonderful foster mom and dad along with foster brothers. The foster mom and dad showed him that they were there to encourage him to become a good adult. Also to give back what was given to him a home with loving parents. My success was that I had complete support from Donald Stewart my husband and our two children Shalanda and DJ. We were a family team.

Caring For Foster Children

The days would begin with my knowing I'm their "fill-in-mom". I would tell the children that as a "fill-in-mom" I would not take their mothers' place but would be there for them. The children would be with our family from six months to a year. When we first began excepting foster children into our home our son was about 10 years old and our daughter was 12 years old. Every day began 5:30 am. I woke up the children they would stay in bed until I knocked on their bedroom doors. Sometimes I have to yell please rise and shine! There would be seven youngsters with us from 6 months to a year which lived in our six bedroom house. Our children welcomed the additions to the family. My husband Stewart had remodeled the first floor of our brick and stone three story apartment house. The back yard was huge. From the deck we could watch the children play. Everyone could eat in the large kitchen.

Since I enjoy cooking everyone would get up when I yelled "rise and shine!" and would be ready to smell the rolls, eggs, bacon, sausage, grits and home fries with onions before leaving for school or for the babysitter. We had seven foster children at a time ranging in ages from one year to fifteen years old. The seven children plus our two children made nine children to get ready each morning. Sometimes siblings would be with us. They would be protective of one another and would help each other get dressed and be ready for the day. The boys always had their own rooms and the girls theirs. Stewart would be the first one home in the afternoon to greet the school aged children and I would collect the younger ones from the babysitter after work. I know what it was like to have a large family coming from one of thirteen and my husband one of fourteen. The kitchen was the heart beat of the home. Supper preparation began five o'clock. I not only cooked southern style but also was required by caseworkers to cook ethic foods for the Haitians, Jamaican, Cuban and Bahamian.

While supper was being prepared older children did their homework. They would help the younger children with theirs if needed. I was involved in the children's school progress by school visits as needed and the supervision of homework. In caring for foster children you must cooperate with the agency that placed the children in your home. Miracle Maker was the agency for our children. To maintain good health each child was taken for routine medical and dental examinations to the appropriate physicians, clinics or hospitals as arranged with the caseworker and discussed treatment and follow-up with the agency worker. We had to advise the agency immediately if health care was needed. Reported immediately all accidents, and illnesses to them as soon as possible or within 12 hours.

We provided adequate or appropriate clothing that would not distinguish the foster child from my children. Each child had individual drawers and closet space for their own clothing and personal care items. Emotional and affection and support were needed for the children because of the emotional abuse the children feels. The children already suffered emotional abuse. A child needs to feel loved. If a parent constantly verbally talks down to a child and never say good things to that child, that child becomes discouraged and will feel as though he or she has failed. Every child needs affection. They need to know that they are being loved and wanted. It is very important to a child. The support we give to a child will go along way such as encouraging that child and assuring him or her that you are there for them no matter what happens. Many of my foster children had such disrupted lives such as physical neglect lack of shelter, care and supervision of parents. Some felt their mothers put a man before them and put them on the side. Each child that was placed in our home was told that I am a fill-in-mom for them and I am not trying to take their mothers place.

One thing I asked them to do was to go to church and it was discussed and all agreed to go. They were all in the church choir. The church choir welcomed their voices. They enjoyed being in the choir as well. The older children enjoyed bowling and movies. After all is said and done these children found a welcoming place in our home.

When our biological son graduated from high school he came to Stewart and I and said he was going into the marines and wanted to know how to contact his birth parents. We were astonished. It appears the girls including his own sister had told him he was a foster child that was adopted by us.

The B Boys

On February 18, 1988 the B brothers came to live with us. This was the first time they had ever been placed in a foster home. They were afraid because they had never been away from their parents before and did not know what to expect in the new home. The B brother's ages were two, six, seven, and thirteen. Gene was a two year old who was a very active child. He was lovable and loved to play but he was an asthmatic. Ernie was a six year old little shy boy. He was a child who always had a smile on his face. He loved to play with cars. He loved to eat. He was a friendly little boy who got along with the other boys in the home. He loved to sing and his favorite song was Thumbelina.

One day we put fruits on the table Ernie saw the fruits and decided to ease his way to the table where the fruits were. Ernie would take a grape from the fruit bowl while watching to see if anyone was looking at him taking grapes. He would take grapes put them in his mouth as fast as he could so that no one he thought would see him doing that. I would see him out of the corner of my eyes, not letting him know I was watching him. The fruits were for everyone but little Ernie did not realize he didn't have to take the grapes like that; all he had to do was just ask for them. The other brothers were Al and Joe.

Al was a seven year old who was not friendly at first. He had to adjust to his surroundings and especially since he was in a different home. Once he warmed up to everyone in the home, he was out going and didn't care if he was right or wrong. It took longer for Al to become comfortable in the home. Al would fight with Ernie or anyone who got in his way. Al did not adjust to being away from his parents as fast as Ernie did. Al was angry due to not understanding that this was a home for him only a short while. Al and Ernie were very close. They finally learned how to trust us. Al had a good spirit and I know he loved his family and friends. Al was killed 6-23-06 in Brooklyn N.Y. at the age of twenty five. He will be missed. The person that killed him was caught.

Joe was thirteen was like a father to Al, Ernie and Gene. He looked after his brothers and was concerned about their well being. Joe is well loved by all who really got to know him. He has a caring spirit and only wanted the best for his siblings. He learned at an early age how to work on cars. He was always helping someone in need. Joe accepted us as his parents and showed respect for our family as a whole. Joe accepted our children as his brother and sister. He never made any difference in the siblings. He calls Stewart dad to this day and have never called anyone else dad but Stewart.

Joe got married August 12, 2007 the ceremony was done by his dad Stewart who is a minister. All of the B brothers have children accept Al. There was appointed and time that the B brothers were placed in a different foster home with a new foster mother. She was a good foster mother to them. She loves them just as much as I do. After the B brothers were placed there we still saw each other. They are doing well. Their mother is in their lives. She's doing extremely well. We all still keep in touch and see each other when we can.

KG

KG came to us in March of 1988.He was the fourth foster child that entered our home. He was a three year old little boy. He was very bright for his age as well as being comical. KG made everyone in the house laugh. He asked a lot of question. To know him was to love him. He only stayed a short while but had a big impact on us all. He loved to talk and tell you how his day was at the babysitter. When he came from the babysitter he always had something funny to say. He had a good appetite. Every night before he went to bed we would teach him how to say his prayer. Once he learned how to say his prayers he would pray for everyone out loud when he finished he would yell to everyone by name and say good night. We started calling him John boy form the Walton's.

In August of 1988 KG was taken back to his mother and grandmother. This was a sad day for all the children as well as me and Stewart. KG had everyone crying when he left. He didn't want to leave Stewart who he called dad. He wanted Stewart to go with him. Everyone was crying including his siblings that was waiting in the car for him. They began to cry because KG was crying. The caseworker, driver and all around him was crying. There was not a dry eye in the house. When KG got into the car he said "Don't take me from my daddy No. Please." I was all choked up and tried to fight back the tears hearing this coming from a little three year old boy. As we watched the car drive away we all were sad. The children left behind cried their selves to sleep.

KG was the youngest in the home. His mother was a Caucasian woman, and his father was African American man that was in prison. His mother was a prostitute and she had taught him some behaviors that were not appropriate. His sister was in a home across the street from us. He got to see his sister every week. His brothers were placed not close to us. Their behaviors were a problem. We worked on KG so that he would be respectable. We did not want him to show us and other children what he had been taught. The six months he was with us he did improve. Being around Stewart was a positive change for him. I do not know what ever became of him. However I am sure that he will remember the positive things he was taught.

Reese B

Reese came to live with us in 1988. She arrived in the evening. She came in with a smile on her face. She was a tall brown skin girl. She was nine years old but very tall for her age. She was placed due to being sexually abused. She was often left home with her teenage uncles at night while her aunt worked. Reese's aunt left her sons to watch her not aware that her sons were doing more than watching Reese. When she came into our home I was not aware at first she was sexually abused. However the caseworker did not tell me she was sexually abused until I started to watch some of her behaviors.

I started to notice her staying in the bathroom to long. So I decided to go in to see what she was doing to my surprise she was sitting on the toilet playing with herself that is not normal for a nine year old girl. Well so I thought to myself. I asked permission to take her to the doctor to see what was really going on. After taking her to the doctor I was told she had been touched. This little girl had been sexual active. She didn't realize what was happening to her. She would get out the bed at night and crawl to the next room where the boys slept in our home. She would wait until my daughter went to sleep. I could hear the boys all yelling at the same time saying she was trying to feel them. I told the boys whenever she came to their room just call me or yell as loud as they could. They surely yelled very loud and I would come running down the hallway to find her in their room.

I finally asked if she could be removed because I worked and could not get enough sleep at night due to watching her until she went to sleep. It was not fair to the other children in the home to be afraid to go to sleep. Unfortunately she was an innocent little girl caught up in a situation that she should not have been in. The agency removed her and put her in another foster home. My heart went out to her and I wished I could have helped her but it was not easy for me. I had to keep the other children safe especially the boys.

TD

On 3-22-1988 TD entered our home. She was an angry child. She didn't want to be there. She wanted to be with her aunt and uncle. She was twelve years old and was use to being on her own. She didn't like you telling her what to do. She didn't like taking baths. She didn't like washing her clothes and didn't want you to wash them. She would hide her dirty underwear under the carpet in her bedroom. After a while you start smelling this odor and didn't know where the odor was coming from in the room. We started to search to see where the smell was coming from. Finally after moving the furniture in the room we found dirty underwear placed under the carpet where her bed was. She didn't get along with the other girls in the home because one she didn't want to be there and two she was not a clean girl. The other girls were clean and they couldn't take her filth. While being there her mother died and I went with her to her mother funeral. Shortly after her mother funeral her uncle took her and I never heard from her again.

Three Jamaican
LKOE Children

Three Jamaican children came to us in 1988. They were well behaved. You could see they were taught how to behave when in the presence of others. These children were placed because their father was abusive to their mother and not them. They were not allowed to stay in that environment it was not good for them to see their parents acting in such a violent way. The children were brought up in church. Their mother took them to church on Sundays and whenever there were services. The LKOE children stayed with us nearly a year. They adjusted well with us for this to be their first time in foster care.

We were happy to see how the children were getting along with our children. The oldest was a girl; she was eleven year old when she came to us. Her brothers were nine and two. The nine year old boy was quiet. He listens to his sister when she spoke to him very well. He would help around the house. He played with our son very well. He did not disrespect me or my husband at all. He is a young adult with a baby of his own. He is working and doing well for himself.

The two year old boy became attached to us. As a little child the two year old played well and got along with all in the house. He was friendly and loved to play with his toys. When he returned home to his mother I don't know what happen but I was told he said "to his mother I want to go back home to my own mother. In his mind I was his mother. He is now married and is doing fine.

The oldest girl lived with me after she became an adult. She lived upstairs on the fourth floor in our large one family home. We got along well for a while but one day I spoke to her concerning too much traffic going up stairs late at night. She got angry with and said "you just wait and see". She never disrespected me before so I was surprise she made that statement. She was always over protective of me. She would not let anyone raise their voice at me if she heard it, it would be a problem. I treated her as if she was my own flesh and blood. I was attached to her and loved her as if I gave birth to her.

One day after speaking to her about too much traffic going up stairs she got angry. Her company had to pass my bedroom in order to get to up stairs to her place. There was only one way to come in and go out to where she lived. She would play her music very loud this caused a problem because we had to get up early in the morning. Sometime she would just be going to bed when we had to get up. My husband would get up around four o'clock in the morning. He would leave the house about five a.m. and sometimes her company was coming down the stairs about the same time he's leaving for work. It became too much for us to deal with and there were other children in the home at this time. We couldn't have this to continue to go on so we asked her to find somewhere else to live. She got mad with me again and decided she was going to get even with me. She said to me "one day you are going to get it just wait and see. I didn't know what she meant until later on.

One day I received a call from ACS. Apparently she called in a report on me saying I was beating a child that we had adopted and that he had marks all over his body where I beat him. She said I locked him in his room. A caseworker was sent out with in twenty four hours of this report. The case worker checked this little boy and found no marks on him. Caseworker also found there was no door to his room. She reported this to Administration Children's Services (ACS) this was the agency where I worked for thirty five years. My director called me in his office said he had received a report on me concern child abuse, asked if it was true. I told him this was not true but he told me I had to take time off until the investigation on me was over. I had to use my own time that I had acquired. Thank God I had enough time on the books to carry me until this investigation was over. If I had not, what would I have done to take care of my family? My husband was on unemployment. My mortgage had to be paid, food for the children had to still be brought and my other bills needed to be paid. However the agency found the charges that were made against me unfounded. She finally left the home a year later.

While on my way home one day I saw her. I asked her why she did this to me. She replied "I wanted to hurt you because nothing seems to bother you; you act as if you are made out of iron." She asked me to forgive her. I know I must forgive because the bible tells me so. If I don't forgive according to the word then I won't be forgiven by my heavenly father when I ask forgiveness. She broke my heart especially when this little boy did no wrong to her and the caseworker had to check his body because of an untruth. My heart was broken because this shouldn't have happen to this child or me.

All I tried to do was help her in life. I gave her a good home when she needed one. When this happen I could not believe this was happening to me even though she called in a case on her own mother. I never thought it would happen to the one who took her in raised her as my own. I loved her as if she was mine. I pray no one will go through this after all you have done to do right. She deeply hurt me. I could have lost my job, my children, all I worked hard for. It is still painful but I am a survivor. I can do all things through Christ which strengthen me.

She is now working taken care of three daughters. Her oldest daughter is eighteen and will be going to college. She is still at home with her mother and listens to her mother as a young adult should. All of her daughters are said to be fine and doing well.

SEB

SB and sister EB came into foster care on April 24, 1989. This ten year old boy who came into our home had a loud mouth and wanted to fight everyone who looked his way. He came in saying what he wasn't going to take mess from me or anyone else in the home. He was very disrespectful to me, the teachers, principal, students and the school bus drivers. When he went to school he got into trouble soon as he reached the school yard. I would receive a phone call every day concerning his behavior. He was in a special ED class due to his behavior. He would come home and start with everyone in the home. Telling them he was going to kick them or tell them to shut up. He was a bully. Then he would start laughing loud and pointing at them.

No one wanted to be around SB. He would tell me I couldn't cook and that the food wasn't fit to eat but yet he ate the food. He would say to me Ms Stewart you show is fat and ugly, look at you. Then he would start to laugh real loud pointing at me yelling you really is fat and ugly ha-ha. I would tell him you better stop being fresh. In this house we don't disrespect each other. He would laugh even louder still pointing and repeating his remarks.

One day I was held by gun point at my job. When I came home and he found out what happen to me. He wanted to go to my job and find them. He said that no one was supposed to mess with me but him. This is when I knew he really did care.

Now his sister EB she was also in a special education program. She would put her brother up to doing her dirty work. She would sit on the sofa give orders to SB to bring her a soda or fruit. EB loved to eat and never clean up after herself. She just sit on the sofa give orders look at everyone as if they were from another planet then finally ask for more food. She enjoyed playing with my daughter. They would sit in the room with dolls combing their hair all day if they could. My daughter saw her around the area where she lives. She said she looked well. I don't know what ever happened to SB.

TB-Screaming Mimi

On 4-16-1990 a tall slim thirteen year old girl by the name of TB came to live with us temporary. TB loved to laugh. She came from another foster home in which she was placed. She was a nervous wreck. Everything made her nervous. If you looked at her to hard she became nervous and said "What" what did I do now." Then she would start to polish her nails. All of a sudden you would here her yell did you see what I saw? She said "she saw from the corner of her eyes "It was a little red man with a little red nose and a little red hat. She would come running through the house screaming I really saw a little red man with a little red nose and a little hat. She asked everyone did you see him too. The answer everyone would give her was we didn't see it. When she didn't get her way, she would sit in her room and scream CWA. Then say she is calling CWA. After her performance she would sit in the room and read. TB would watch TV with the other children.

TB loved to run away from home but always returned. TB was attached to her grandmother. She felt that her grandmother was the only one that loved her. Her grandmother visited her at the foster care agency every two weeks. She looked forward to a visit with her grandmother. When TB turned eighteen she went to live with her grandmother. She is currently living on her own with an eight year old daughter. She is in college. We are very much in contact. She calls and visits often.

PB-Loner and MP-Petite

On 6-6-1991 PB and MP came into foster care for the first time. They lived with their parent. Both were born in Haiti. They came to the United States to live with their parents. PB which I will refer to as loner. She is called loner because she choose to be left alone. She wanted to stay by herself. She always wanted things her way. Loner often got in to fights with Petite. She always liked to look nice. She would spend hours in the mirror fixing her hair in different styles. I didn't have too many problems with loner. I did want her to feel like she was a part of the family. Loner is now married and has two daughters. She completed college and is teaching in public schools in N.Y.C. She keeps in touch with me.

MP known as petite was a petite brown skin fifteen year old girl born in Haiti and adopted by her aunt at age nine. She is loveable and easy going child. She loves to help do things in the home. She would always volunteer to do everyone else chores in the home. She would ask to rub my feet every day when I arrive in the house and finish dinner. She would say I know you had a hard day at work so sit down and let me do your feet. One day one of the girls hit petite in the head with a wooden hair brush she fell back on the bed in my daughter room for a minute got up and told TB she was going to kill her. TB started to run down the hallway screaming and petite was right behind her. This is when we found out she had a demonic spirit within her. Petite lives in PA with her husband and two children. She is doing fine at this time. She keeps in touch with me.

MP'S Demoniac Spirit

There was a young girl who came to our home at the age of fifteen; she showed signs of being possessed. In the bible there were two demon possessed men who were violent. This is found in Matthew 8:28 also in Matthew 15:22 there was a Canaanite woman who had a daughter suffering from demon possession. This was in the beginning of time and still excise today. This young girl MP was Haitian. She came to N.Y.C. from Haiti in 1985 to live with her aunt and uncle. She was placed in foster care, where she stayed for about two and half years. She was placed in my home because of abuse. Her aunt adopted her when she was nine years old. Her aunt went to Haiti, saw her and fell in love with this little girl. So the aunt decided to take and raise her as her own daughter. Her aunt never had children of her own.

This fifteen year old girl who was born in Haiti is the third child of her mother. Her mother had five daughters. She saw her mother twice in her life. She is a very sweet young girl, very helpful and was loved by all of us. Even though the children loved her, they were afraid when she went through her changes. When she came to our home we were not told that she had any kind of problem. One night one of the girls hit her in the head while playing around with a wooden hair brush. This is when it all began with her having headaches. The headaches became bad. When she got these headaches, she would go through changes especially when the other children began to play noisily, laugh too loud or start to tease her. In school her classmates started acting up or being too noisy it was too much for her, she would get somewhat out of control. The teachers would try to calm her down but it came to appoint where they had to call me at work, to ask me to talk to her. Her teacher said she began to act in a weird way and her voice changed. She became a different person. The teacher began to be afraid of her.

At home one night Screamy Mimi hit her in the head with a wooden hair brush while playing around in my daughter bedroom. She fell back on the bed holding her head, got up talking with a demonic voice and said to Screamy Mimi I am going to kill you. She chased Screamy Mimi down the hallway, away Screamy Mimi came running and screaming petite is after me. This is the name we are calling her. We are calling her this name because she is small dainty trim four feet young lady. Petite was trying to get to Screamy Mimi but I came rushing down the hallway to see what was going on, and to my surprise I saw Petite as a different person. She was talking in a demonic voice. I didn't understand what she was saying. She went to her bedroom laid on her bed holding her head. All of a sudden you could see a hand print around her throat. Her hands were on the bed beside her. There were hands around her throat and they weren't her hands. This was a scary moment.

I had never experience anything like this before. She began to cry out for help, as if someone was chocking her and would say in a low voice please help me. In a low voice she would continue to call out for help. I was surprise to see these hands around her throat and nobody along with these hands. I stood there for a moment in shock. I knew I had to do something so I quickly jumped on the bed where she laid and began to pray. As I prayed the demonic voice said to me "not tonight". I told all the children in the bedroom to get out their bible and hold on to their bibles, and then I told them to leave the room. This demonic spirit was very powerful and didn't give up so easy. I still stayed on the bed praying until the lord delivered me and her. This demonic spirit tired me out but I couldn't give up then. I put a bible on her and a cross in the room. This little leather bible I had given her was found floating in the toilet none of the pages were wet. We never found the cross. This happened at least three times in two years she was with us.

The rest of the girls would put plastic bags around their beds so if she got up they would know and run to get help. Another time during one of her headache spells, she tried to kill herself. She took a butcher knife and put the knife in the middle of her chest. I went behind her and with all of my strength kept her from hurting herself. She had one hand on the butcher knife and I had my hand over her other hand trying to keep her from putting the knife to her chest. I called my husband he had to break the knife in half so she wouldn't hurt herself. Luckily with his military training he could do this.

Another time I had to call the police to help us get her out of the bathroom because she locked the bathroom door and wouldn't let anyone in. She was supposed to be taking a shower. When the police came we got the door open. They found her standing in the bathtub with all her clothes on.

She began to laugh. The police officers were very afraid. They put her in a straight jacket. She came out of the straight jacket like it was a regular coat and gave it back to the police officer with another strange laugh. They were shocked and so were we. She began hitting the police officers with one finger and was able to knock them against my hallway wall at that time they wanted to use their stun guns but I begged them not too. I then called a detective who the family knew. He stood with me until the ambulance came again. She went quietly with them. During this time our daughter fainted then went into a seizure. She too went by ambulance. The second teenager was also affected by this occurrence and she had to be transported to the hospital all were checked by the doctor. All the girls came home and went to bed. Next morning everybody went to school. No one wanted to stay home.

The next incident happened in church and fortunately our caseworker and director of the program were there too. That Sunday morning service was good, choir singing, people shouting and praising God, all of a sudden she began to praise God, the drums were beating, the piano was playing, she fell out and something once again took control of her. She started to talk in a demonic voice, the preachers gathered around her, my pastor at that time started to pray for her then this voice said to him "Not today old man. The preacher asked the voice that came from petite "who are you?

The voice replied. "Eladiac" or something to that effect. So the pastor spoke to the voice coming from petite and said come out but the pastor was unable to cast this voice out. It was as if there was another person inside her speaking. She pulled the pastor to her and began to choke him with his own tie. Others tried to help but they couldn't. I went to her and hit her on the bottom of her feet this caused her to pass out in the choir stand.

One of the church deacons from Barbados said he could help her. She began to crawl on her stomach like a snake and flipped over on her back. She hit the deacon where it hurt the most and he ran out the church holding his private parts. The congregation followed. There were a few people left behind. Someone had called the police, the police came asked what kind of church is this. I replied Pentecostal. The police called for an ambulance. She was put in the ambulance and taken to Woodhull Hospital where she stayed for two weeks to be watched but nothing happen in the hospital. They had her under watch care. I went to see her; the voice came again and said to me "Do you think I am crazy"? I am not going to act up in here. She returned back home with me from the hospital because she was still in my care. She stayed with us for a little while longer. It came time that she had to leave because this voice came again and said to me if I don't let her go it would destroy my home. She was placed in another home at my request. I didn't want her to go but I knew I had too. The next home that took her in experienced this voice and her foster mother was given my number to call me to ask what to do. My advice at that time was to back off and let her calm down even though she was destructive. I then realized that the agency does not tell you everything about the children being placed in your home.

This was an experience that I will never ever forget. I call this a mother's love because you have to love a child that you didn't give birth to. I knew with Christ in my life that I can do all things. Without having Christ in my life I would not have made it and still be in my right mind. There is something we can't do alone. I know there is someone bigger than I.

SJ-Scared Stiff

SJ a Jamaican young girl who entered into our home as a teenager. She came in angry at the world. She had come from another foster home. Coming from the foster home she was in, she was angry and didn't believe that she was going to be treated right in our home. The first foster home she was in, she was unhappy and wasn't treated fairly. She came with some baggage that had to be addressed. She was given her own bedroom when she first arrived.

After being there for a while two sisters came and she shared a bedroom with them. There was an adjustment period that took place within her. She overcame some of her anger. She went to church every Sunday, sang in the choir. She went to school. She started to show some progress in her ways of thinking and handling situations in the home. She showed respect for our family. Our daughter and her looked alike. Sometime if we took a quick look we got the wrong child. She was very helpful around the house. She showed me how to prepare Jamaican food such as plantains, curry chicken etc. She was with us a while. She accepted us as her family and we accepted her as our own child. Her mother is in her life. Her mother came to visit her when she was in care. She sometimes she went to spend the weekend with her mother and grandmother. She enjoyed spending time with her grandmother. She would tell us stories about her grandmother that was interesting.

One day while setting in her bedroom a strange thing happen that she couldn't believe her eyes. Petite her roommate started to act strange. She got scared of what she was seeing take place with petite so she had to be taken to the hospital by ambulance. When the ambulance people came into her room, they asked her what the problem was. She said "she felt like someone was holding her legs down and she couldn't move. She was put on the stretcher and took to the hospital to be evaluated by a doctor. She was seen by a doctor and sent home. She got married. She has three children. She is doing well. She didn't forget her teaching that was instilled in her while living with us. We keep in touch and see each other when we can. I will never forget her and she will always be in my heart.

Scared Stiff View on What Happen at the Stewart home

————— ⟠ —————

Growing up in the Stewart's home was very different from where she had lived before. She had lived other places but nothing ever had happen like this: She shared a room with petite not knowing that petite had an issue. She remembered when she first met petite. One of her siblings told her to stay away from petite because when she got a headache, she was out of control.

Looking back at what my siblings were trying to tell me I never really understood why until one day I saw for myself what they meant. I saw petite lying on her bed in her room we shared, I asked her are you okay? She replied in a deep rusty voice "leave me alone". She sounded like a very angry man. I remember feeling scared and puzzled but I turned and walked away. I remember thinking to myself, that's not the petite I thought I knew. That same day another sibling walked in the room and asked if petite was okay and petite replied yes in a baby sweet voice. Then she got up off the bed said she was going to take a shower.

It was then something happen to me, I had a premonition of everything that was about to happen. After she went to the bathroom a few minutes later I heard yelling. I saw daddy Stewart running to the bathroom where petite was and mommy Stewart was trying to help another sibling who fainted. Mommy Stewart kept trying to revive the sibling that had fainted. At this time petite was still in the bathroom speaking like a man and foaming from the mouth. Something inhuman was inside of petite. She kept telling mommy Stewart she could make the other sibling who fainted better if mommy Stewart would tell her she loved her.

The same day the police were called to the home and the ambulance took a sibling to the hospital while petite was fighting with the police officers, they could not bring her uncontrolled. She was about 4'11 inches tall and about 110 pounds. There were four police officers but somehow petite looked to have been stronger. Finally she was put in a straight jacket but do you know she came out of the straight jacket and gave it to the police laughing loud and hitting them with one finger knocking them against the hallway wall.

The police officers looked confused. They couldn't believe what they were seeing. Looking back, the police officers were afraid. After that happen I never wanted to sleep in the room with her again. What bothered me the most was the evil that existed in her. The home we lived, I know God was there with us. We went to church every Sunday. I was born in the West Indies so as a child I would hear stories of voodoo and evil but I never believed it. I don't think any human being really wants to believe that evil can exist in another human being, and for one I didn't until I met petite. SJ.

The Six "Y" Children who
Four Names began with "M"
One with "S" and one with "K"

The six Y children came January 5, 1993. They all had problem some worse than others. Where do I began with them, it is so much to be said. Well I will began with the oldest girl MY, she was overly protective of her siblings. She didn't want me to do anything for her or her siblings. She was like a mother hen watching your every move. She watched everything that I did or did not do. If it wasn't what she thought I was supposed to do, she would sneak and call the caseworker on me or wait until their visit at the agency to report me. The visits were every two weeks where family members were to come and visit them. There were some disappointments when their uncle did not show up. When no one showed up for them after sitting at the agency for one hour or more they became angry especially the oldest girl. She didn't want to listen anyway so this gave her an excused to really act out. They were allowed to go and stay with their uncle once a month. When their uncle did not show up it would break their heart and I knew I was in for a rough week with them.

Every two weeks their uncle would come to visit them at the agency, because this would help him to get them when it was time for them to be release. When they would go to the uncle house they would take my cook books without permission. When I was looking for my cook book to make something special for them the books were gone. I would ask if anyone had seen my books they would say no. The children had a good appetite. If the first child got angry she didn't want her siblings to eat until she said so but it didn't work that way for her. The first child would call all of her siblings in the room they slept in when she was upset with me. After a while the siblings stop listen to her they became comfortable with us and knew we only wanted the best for them. The first child didn't want to listen at all. She wouldn't come straight home from school or go straight to the babysitter after school. She played in the park with her friends. She was only eleven years old. She would curse at the babysitter and refuse to do anything the babysitter told her to do. When the babysitter told her she was going to tell me what she did or said. She would say "so what" she can't do anything. She said my uncle said to tell him and he would deal with her. She would curse in the home throw things in the room until she decided to go to bed.

The second girl wanted to listen to me but again the first girl would step in and start to fight with her telling her she had to listen to her because she was the oldest and I was not their mother. The second girl was a quiet little girl and did well in class. She tried really hard to do right. She is married now and has a son. She went to college and finished.

The third girl was out of control. She would fight and get suspended from school. She would go to school and make her classmates the girls sit on the window seal in the classroom. She would go to the bathroom in school and if there were girls in the bathroom she would make them sit on the toilet until she said get off the toilet seat. The girls in the class were afraid of her. The teachers was always calling me at work to come to school for her behavior. She was an angry child. She knew she couldn't beat her sisters so she took it out on others.

Fourth child was a boy. He also had issues, would get angry and bite all of his siblings. He would take their feet and bite them. I would hear the siblings yelling stop. The fourth child would then go to his baby brother grab his feet and bite it. I would hear the sound coming from the baby boy" ebb or a bird sound as if a bird was singing. He would bite the door frame; you could see teeth marks all around the door frame. He would bite his wooden frame bed or anything he saw with wood. He would bite my car seat while taking him to the babysitter along with whoever was setting next to him in the car. He would often get upset with his siblings while riding to the babysitter. He had no special person to bite. On his good day he would help around the house. He called me mommy and would say "mommy me will do it for you". He liked sweeping the floor or trying to dust. He wanted to help on his good days.

Fifth child is a boy. He was four years old. He is a loveable little boy. He was a follower whatever he saw someone else do he would try it too. The sixth child was a little boy. He was a happy little boy with a smile always on his face. He played with the other boys in the house. He played with his toys and tried to stay out of the reach of his brother that loved to bite people. They are all young adults now and doing well.

Shouting John

I met shouting John through my daughter. He went to the same school she attended. He was in foster care with someone else. He lived down the street from us. He lived in a big black and white house with some other foster children. He went to church faithfully with his foster mother who was a pastor. He was not happy with the home he lived in. He would come to our home after school shouting as he walked through the door. Shouting after he is walking out the door. He never stopped shouting. I don't know how he could shout from morning, noon and night. He always has a smile on his face regardless of what he is going through. At the age of twelve he began preaching. He needed a place to live and I said that he could stay with us. He was always in church. I didn't have to wonder where he was. He could be found in a church not far from us. When he came home from wherever he had been, he would come in shouting making his way up stairs as he is going up stairs he is banging on the banishers as if he is beating a drum not missing one beat with his feet. Singing as he goes up the steps come and dine the master is calling. This was an every day event for shouting john. He loves to praise the lord. He is now married with four girls. He is a Bishop and has started his own church. He loves people and loves to be around his family and friends. He has come a long way and I am proud of him. We see each other often.

My Daughter Shalanda Account

My mother asked my brother and I how would we feel about foster children. At first I really didn't know what to think. I did want to have sisters. I wasn't too interested in having any more brothers. When the first set of children came to our home it was boys. How can I play with boys? My brother enjoyed being with them we all began to bond with one another. Then the next child came and it was another boy he was two years old, I fell in love with this child and I wanted him to stay forever. Then finally a 2 girl's one was crazy and the other one really did not want to be bothered. So now I'm thinking what my parents get themselves into. Eventually the crazy girl left she was placed somewhere else. It was then that my mother explained that she wasn't crazy she had been sexually abused. So now I'm thinking wow a lot of these children have some serious problems. I realized then how blessed I was to have both of my parents all though my mother was the strictest women in the world I wouldn't change them for nothing in the world.

I remember the night that the 2 year old had to go back to his mom. That devastated all of the kids in the house. It was like someone ripped a piece of our heart out. Everyone was up late crying. I saw him as the case worker came and carried him outside. He kept crying saying "don't take me from my daddy" "Please that's my daddy". I think even the case workers were getting emotional. What could you do? We all knew that the children didn't come to stay. After that moment I vowed not to get attached to any other child. From the time that KG left there were a many other children that came and left. Finally some girls that were my age. Then some more girls. I was so happy. I figured we would go to school together and do everything together. My mother did not think that it was a good idea to have us all in the same school. She said that that would be trouble. So my mother had us separated two girls per school. I guess she thought it would keep us out of trouble, but it didn't.

I had so much fun with my sisters. Although we had different parents and came from different backgrounds we felt like blood sisters. I remember my mother telling us that we could go out one weekend a month without her. Oh what joy that was, however there was always a catch with my mother. She wanted us home by 7pm. That time was a good time to come home but it had to be exactly 7pm. The first weekend we chose we went to the movies on our way back home the train was delayed. By this time we all were scared. When Velma Stewart said be home a 7pm she meant that. We all ran from Halsey Street train station to Jefferson Avenue where we lived. To our surprise we made it on time exactly 7pm. When we entered the second door to enter the apartment wouldn't you know my mother was standing at the door. She had her hands on her hips and her feet tapping. From the look on her face she was not happy. She said it's

7:01 you're late. Our reply was ma we are here on time. She said you should already be in the apartment at 7:00 not at the door. We were on punishment for that one minute. I could not believe it. My mother was so strict that we could not sit outside by ourselves she had to be present. When the boy even looked at us she would tell them to get lost.

I now realize why she had to be strict. Raising seven teenage girls with raging hormones was not easy. She felt like she had to be the warden in order to keep us in place. All of us are glad that she was strict it now allows us to be better parents to our children. Our children will have the same respect for us as we had for her. My father was the easy going dad. He would let us get away with a lot of things. He is every child's dream father. I'm glad we had balance in our home because if both parents were strict I probably would have wanted to live with one of my father's sisters.

What can I say about my sisters? Well LE and I were once close until she disrespected my parents now we are in our separated lives I do keep in contact with her children. PB is still a loner so we do not have a relationship with each other but I still love her. Although MP had her demonic attacks I still loved her. Living with her was an experience that you would never forget. In fact people do not believe the things that we experienced any way so I don't even bother to tell them. Demons are real, evil is real and it lived at 911 Jefferson avenue. It was so bad that the police knew our address by heart. TB,SJ and my self are close to each other we speak all the time. As far as the boys go Joe and I are the closest that's my big brother we are inseparable. I could not ask for a better set of siblings I would never change anything from my child hood.

How I Over Came

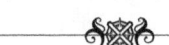

Being a foster mother was an experience I will never forget. So many times I have dealt with children of different cultural and racial backgrounds when I worked at ACS. It can become challenging when you have children in your home that are all different ages with mental and physical needs. Sometimes they would bicker and argue. I had to always remember that they had their own different personalities along with their likes and dislikes. I was able to deal with each child that came to us. It did not matter what their previous family life was like. I've learned that no matter who you are or where you come from each child need to feel loved by us. Just to think most of theses children were physically and mentally abused but they still had a great love for their parents. They all cried out for someone, somewhere to accept them and called them as if they were their own. There were tears but we all over came.

The children I took care of are all grown hopefully they are now instilling the same morals and values I showed them in into their own children. I would never tell anyone that being a foster mother is easy. It is not in any way easy you not only have to deal with the children's personalities but also the parents. However it is rewarding to see the children you raised become beautiful adults with children. I still get calls for birthdays, and holidays along with pictures from the children of their families. My husband and I have made it through the storm. We made it through the rough demonic forces that could have taken over our home. We overcame. I firmly believe that God was watching over our family. The children feel free to be themselves, love themselves, and help themselves. We have done our job. We met ever goal that was set for the children under our roof. It is only in looking back and remembering that we realize we have accomplished so much.